STUCK LOVING ME

Understanding the True Nature

of

Narcissism

AshleyRai Talley

Dedication

This book is dedicated to all the women who have survived and overcome abuse in any form—the ones who found their strength in silence and the ones still searching for their voice. To those who have been too afraid to tell their story, know that your truth matters, your pain is valid, and your healing is possible. May you find the courage to choose yourself, the strength to break free, and the love that has always been within you.

You are not alone. You are worthy. You are enough.

Table of Acts

Act 1

INTRODUCTION 1

INCEPTION 4

REFLECTIVE INTERMISSION

THE BACKDROP 12

REFLECTIVE INTERMISSION

Act 2

THE ANTAGONIST 17

THE PROTAGONIST 29

Act 3

REFLECTIVE INTERMISSION

THE SUPPORTING CAST 44

THE CLIMAX 49

INSIDE-OUT ACTING 55

CURTAIN SPEECH 64

THE ENCORE 66

Introduction

Why Shed Light

Narcissism is a term often thrown around casually today, used to describe individuals who seem excessively self-centered or vain. However, the true nature of narcissism, particularly narcissistic personality disorder (NPD), is far more complex and deeply rooted in psychological pathology. In this book, we will delve into the intricacies of narcissism, exploring its origins, manifestations, and impacts on both the individuals who exhibit these traits and those who interact with them.

My journey with narcissism is not merely academic; it is deeply personal. I have spent years grappling with the reality of having a close relationship with a narcissist. The emotional rollercoaster, the constant manipulation, and the erosion of my self-worth have left indelible marks on my life. Through this book, I aim to provide a comprehensive understanding of narcissism, drawing from both extensive research and my own lived experiences. From the outside, a narcissist can seem charming, confident, and charismatic. They often excel professionally and socially, leaving others in awe of their apparent success. However, beneath this polished exterior lies a fragile self-esteem, an insatiable need for admiration, and a lack of genuine empathy. The dichotomy between the narcissist's public persona and private behavior can be bewildering and devastating for those who are close to them.

In the next chapters, we will delve into what narcissism really is, starting with the psychology behind it and then exploring specific tactics narcissists use to manipulate and control others. We'll also discuss the long-term effects of narcissistic abuse and share practical ways to heal and take back control of your life.

It has not been easy sharing my story because it requires revisiting painful memories and confronting some harsh realities about my past. But I believe that by sharing, I can help others who might be going through something similar. The first step in breaking free from narcissism is understanding it—and that's how you start reclaiming your true self.

This book is for anyone who's ever felt trapped in a narcissist's web of lies and deceit, those who are trying to understand their behavior, and the friends and family members seeking to support their loved ones. With the right knowledge, empathy, and resilience, you can break free from the shadows of narcissism and find your way to healing and self-worth.

Come along with me as we unravel the complexities of narcissism, expose hidden truths, and pave the way for a healthier, more authentic life.

Inception

Origin of Narcissism

The nature of narcissism, with its intense and often theatrical presentation, lends itself perfectly to this format. Each chapter feels like a scene in a play, letting us uncover the layers of narcissism in a way that pulls you in and keeps you engaged.

The term 'narcissism' originated from the story of Narcissus and Echo in *Ovid's Metamorphoses* (Book 3), written in the first century. Back then, it was more of a myth, but over time, it's developed into a specialized psychoanalytic term. In the myth, Narcissus, the son of the river god Cephissus and the nymph Liriope, was known for his striking beauty, which caught the attention of many—one of whom was the nymph Echo. Because of Narcissus's pride and self-love, he never found someone who could truly capture his heart. Along the way, he left behind a trail of heartbroken maidens—and a few young men, too. As a result, the gods punished him by making him fall in love with his reflection in a pool of water. He experienced the deepest form of unrequited love. Realizing that the object of his affection could not return his feelings, he pined away and died. According to the myth, a flower grew in the place where he died, which was named after him – the narcissus.

As I researched the term, I found that Narcissism has a long and complex history in psychology. It originally focused on a type of self-centered sexuality. The first psychologist to mention something similar was Havelock Ellis in 1898, who used the myth of Narcissus to describe a form of "auto-eroticism," where someone becomes excessively fascinated with themselves and their appearance. Sigmund Freud later built on this idea, adding terms like “ego-libido” and “narcissistic libido” between 1905 and 1953, further shaping our understanding of narcissism. He identified narcissism as a normal stage in the development of a child, primary narcissism, and he also recognized secondary narcissism as a pathological form of narcissism in adults. When someone’s libido is turned inward, focusing on themselves rather than others, it can lead to a condition like narcissistic personality disorder. This is often marked by traits such as grandiosity, a constant need for admiration, and a lack of empathy. Another key figure to mention here is the early psychoanalyst Ernest Jones. In his *Essays in Applied Psychoanalysis* (1913-1951), he was the first to interpret narcissism as a personality trait and to introduce the idea of a "god complex."

A *"god complex"* is a pattern in which an individual believes they have great power, ability, infallibility, and influence and are superior to others. They may feel entitled to special treatment and act as though rules don't apply to them. There is a disregard for the needs of others, and they can also become intensely jealous and controlling. They can be standoffish, inaccessible, self-admiring, overconfident, or auto-erotic. There is a high need for uniqueness; they do not want to be compared to anyone else and are offended when compared. It is literally as if they are their god, a kind of self-idolization.

These psychologists were some of the first to study narcissism. But as a follower of God and the author of this book, I'd be doing a disservice if I didn't highlight that God, long before any psychologist or mythological storyteller, warned us about narcissism through the Apostle Paul.

In 2 Timothy, Paul describes the types of people to avoid, providing timeless wisdom on the dangers of narcissistic behavior and its soon noticeable uncovering.

> 2 *Timothy 3:1-9 (amp) "But understand this, that in the last days, dangerous times [of great stress and trouble] will come [will come difficult days that will be hard to bear.] For people will be lovers of self [narcissistic, self-focused], lovers of money [Impelled by greed], boastful, arrogant, revilers, disobedient to parents, ungrateful, unholy and profane, [and they will be] unloving [devoid of natural human affection, calloused, and inhumane], irreconcilable, malicious, gossips, devoid of self-control [intemperate, immoral], brutal, haters of good, traitors, reckless, conceited lovers of [sensual] pleasures rather than God, holding to a form of [outward] godliness [religion], although they have denied its power [for their conduct nullifies their claim of faith]. Avoid such people and keep far away*

from them. For among them are those who worm their way into homes and captivate morally weak and spiritually dwarfed women weighed down by [the burden of their] sins, easily swayed by various impulses, always learning and listening to anybody who will teach them, but never able to come to the knowledge of truth. Just as Jannes and Jambres [the court magicians of Egypt] opposed Moses, so these men also oppose the truth, men of depraved mind, unqualified and worthless [as teachers] in regard to faith. But they will not get far, for their meaningless nonsense and ignorance will become obvious to everyone, as was that of Jannes and Jambres."

Theologian William Barclay, in his commentary on 2 Timothy, points out that the first quality mentioned is a life centered on self. He used the term "*philautos*," which translates to "self-loving." According to Barclay, this self-love is at the root of all other sins. The moment a man makes his own will the center of life, divine and human relationships are destroyed, and obedience to God and charity to men become impossible. The essence of

Christianity is not the enthronement but the obliteration of self.

Before my experience with a Narcissist, I had read these verses in 2 Timothy several times. However, it was not until the Holy Spirit brought this scripture back to my memory that I realized it referred not just to a mental disorder, but to a conscious choice by individuals to center their lives around themselves—an indication of the times and seasons. Paul describes the wicked characteristics of our present time, where both men and women are lovers of self. As believers in Christ, we can identify this level of deception through discernment. At my point of collision with the Narcissist, my discernment was masked by unhealed trauma and pain (spiritually dwarfed).

Through this experience, I learned the importance of allowing God to heal open and exposed wounds so that I would not make decisions from places of depravity but from discernment. We will delve into this more in a later chapter. As I conclude setting the stage, I want to highlight the end of verse 5 and urge you to apply this when encountering these behaviors in relationships with people. Paul warns us to avoid such people, turn away, and keep far from them. Do not be deceived: *“Evil company corrupts good habits.”* (1 Corinthians 15:33)

Reflective Intermission

1. Have you ever noticed any narcissistic behavior in yourself or in the people around you?

2. Reflect on the idea of the *"god complex"* as described in the chapter. How does it challenge your view on power, humility, and entitlement?

3. How does the passage from 2 Timothy 3:1-9 help you see narcissism as more than just a mental condition, but also as a spiritual warning?

4. How can healing help protect you from being manipulated by narcissistic behaviors?

5. In what ways has your healing process improved your ability to discern toxic relationships or unhealthy behaviors?

The Backdrop

"We are pressed on every side by troubles, but we are not crushed. We are perplexed, but not driven to despair. We are hunted down, but not abandoned by God. We get knocked down, but we are not destroyed."

~ 2 Corinthians 4:8-9 NLT

Imagine a grand theater, dimly lit, with thick velvet curtains concealing the world behind them. On the stage, a scene is about to unfold, but this is no ordinary performance. This one is personal. The stakes are high, life or death, and the roles are methodically cast. At the center stage, commanding the spotlight, stands the Narcissist, the story's antagonist. With every gesture and every line, they project charm, confidence, and control, drawing the audience's admiration. What lies beneath this dazzling façade lies the intricate web of manipulation and self-interest, a script they have perfected over time.

The beginning scene appears ordinary to the untrained and undiscerning eye, emotionally alluring. But just offstage, in the shadows, is where the real story is infused. This is the place where the Protagonist, the individual unknowingly caught in the Narcissist's rotation, resides. Initially, they are perceived as happy and willing to play the supporting role in the Narcissist's act. As the story progresses, cracks begin to form. The protagonist finds themselves constantly shifting, adjusting, and bending to the Narcissist's subtly abrupt demands while grappling with an inner confusion that the audience never sees.

This isn't just a one-act show; it's been going on for years. The same scenes keep playing out, only with different supporting characters stepping in, each one naively unaware of their role. With every new act, the Narcissists bring in fresh allies, shifting in and out of the narrative and strengthening their grip. The protagonist is caught between the Narcissist's grand vision and the influence of the supporting cast, often feeling more like a pawn than a partner in this elaborate play.

But it wasn't just a performance; these were the scenes playing out in the theater of my real life. At 34, as I emerged from the wreckage of my second marriage, I was emotionally and spiritually drained- a deficit that ran deeper than I understood at the time. The past year had been one of the hardest, a relentless unraveling. In hindsight, I should have given myself time to heal, to allow space for God to mend the brokenness. But instead, I pushed down the feelings, convinced myself I could "keep it moving," and stepped back onto the stage. That's where my path collided with my protagonist; his charm immediately drew me in. He appeared thoughtful and kind. He listened intently, taking in each detail as though I were the only character in his world. He mirrored my likes, and reflected my interests- it felt like a perfect performance.

As the scenes of the relationship unfolded, however, elusive changes began to appear in his performance. Fleeting moments of control, and hints of manipulation, the changes were small but an undeniable reminder that he held the script. I tried to bring up these troubling cues, hoping to discuss what I saw, but he sidestepped conversations, masking any discomfort with carefully timed gifts. His lavish gestures were the props used to distract me from the shifting scenes of control and inconsistency. What I understand now as 'love bombing' had been his way of keeping me in my role, charmed, uncertain, and still entranced by the person I thought he was.

Reflective Intermission

1. Have you ever felt like you were just playing a part in someone else's story? How did that affect how you see yourself?

2. Healing is crucial before stepping into new relationships. How can you focus on self-care and healing in your own life?

3. Have you ever had someone use gifts or big gestures to manipulate or control you? How can you tell the difference between real love and manipulation disguised as kindness?

4. How do spiritual insight and discernment help you identify when you're being misled or manipulated?

5. Think about how faith can guide you through toxic relationships. How can spiritual growth strengthen your ability to set boundaries and make healthier choices?

The Antagonist

Narcissist, the Lead Character

"Sin whispers to the wicked, deep within their hearts. They have no fear of God at all. In their blind conceit, they cannot see how wicked they really are. Everything they say is crooked and deceitful. They refuse to act wisely or do good."

~ Psalm 36:1-3 NLT

Every theater production has a star, and in this play, the Narcissist stands at the center stage, a master of creating illusions. Commanding the spotlight, the narcissist crafts a persona that is captivating, multi-faceted, and always just out of reach. They are not just any character; they are the director, the lead actor, and the scriptwriter! Behind the charm, the carefully curated charisma, and the deep-seated vulnerability they project, lies a core that is driven by control, self-interest, and a craving for validation.

To truly understand the narcissist's role as an Antagonist, we must explore their calculated behaviors. It's not simply an act but an embodiment with conviction, relying on a predictable, yet delicate script designed to secure the devotion, admiration, and sympathy of those around them.

The Magnetic Mask

At first glance, the narcissist appears magnetic. In the opening scenes, they wear a mask of charm that is almost hypnotic. They exude confidence and appear genuinely interested in others, mirroring their desires, interests, and dreams. It's as if they've tailored themselves to be exactly what their "protagonist" needs, pulling their target into play and onto the stage.

The charm isn't random or genuine; it is a carefully curated act that serves as a gateway. By reflecting the desires and interests of the ensnared, they draw people in, establishing a sense of trust and safety. The target, "the protagonist," becomes convinced they've found someone extraordinary. Someone who understands them like no one else. But the truth of the charm offensive is a strategic move, a performance designed to mesmerize and disarm. It is intended to leave the protagonist feeling seen, heard, and appreciated in ways they had never experienced before.

My antagonists' charm from the beginning had me in a chokehold. He would show up with 'just because' gifts at the most unexpected moments. The thoughtful tokens made me feel deeply valued. He would cook for me, and we would settle in to watch our favorite movies together, sharing quiet, comforting evenings that felt safe and grounding. He was consistent in his attention, offering a listening ear and even helping me express emotions I didn't know how to share. Every action seemed intentional, carefully showing how much, he cared. He attended ministry events with me, showing genuine interest in the things I loved and the people that mattered the most. His dedication felt profound, and we shared some of the same family traumas that seemed to create a unique bond. In those moments, he felt like my partner and my safe place. But I would soon come to understand that his charm, and careful attentiveness, was a much more a crafted performance than genuine affection.

The Intimidation Grip

Once the narcissist has secured the protagonist's trust and sense of safety, the temperament shifts. Beneath the charm, an undertone of intimidation and control begins to emerge. This is usually not overt. Instead, the narcissist uses indirect tactics to establish dominance. There may be subtle criticisms, undermining confidence, or backhanded comments that leave the protagonist questioning their worth.

The transition to intimidation serves as a tool to erode the protagonist's sense of independence. By keeping them slightly off balance, the narcissist reinforces a power dynamic that secures their position at the center of attention. They need the protagonist to feel dependent and anxious with the intent to weaken any challenge to their authority. Some cues you may encounter are sharpened tone, dismissive gestures, pauses that communicate disdain, or days of silence with calculated glances.

The transition to intimidation was so discreet it almost slipped past me. On my 35th birthday, only 3 months after we were dating, I found out

I was pregnant. As my pregnancy went on, I started to notice little cracks in the façade. Sometimes, during conversations, he'd leave the room, his voice quieter, his whole attitude suddenly distant. Whenever I asked him about it, he'd either brush me off with vague excuses or tell me I was overreacting. It was clear to me that some things were no longer for me to know. If I ever dared to challenge his decisions, expensive gifts would appear afterward, a gesture that felt more like an apology until I saw that strings were attached. When I would confront him about it, he would twist the narrative, suggesting that I was ungrateful and unappreciative. "If you don't appreciate it, I won't bother next time," he would say, leaving me feeling guilty and indebted. If he cooked food and I didn't feel like eating it, his response was swift and harsh. "You're so ungrateful," he'd snap, his tone sharp and accusatory, leaving me feeling like a scolded child refusing to eat their vegetables. It was a small moment but one that chipped away at my autonomy.

The cracks in his façade became impossible to ignore the weekend before we were moving in together. He vanished without explanation, only to reappear the following afternoon, as though nothing had happened. When I confronted him by asking him to leave, his demeanor shifted immediately. Defensive words turned into a storm of rage. Before I could process what was happening, he had swept everything off the bar in a violent flourish, the sound of shattering glass hitting the floor. Then, in a terrifying burst of anger, he charged toward me and my daughter, punching a hole in the wall inches away from my face before storming out the door. I stood there, frozen, clutching our daughter as the air hung heavy with disbelief. His most effective weapon was silence. If I pressed too hard or did not do something that he wanted me to do the way he wanted me to do it, he'd disappear- no calls, no texts, no replies, and days of eerie quiet left me feeling abandoned. Then, out of nowhere, he would resume talking as if nothing happened, as if it was me who had been distant. Each time, I felt confused and overwhelmed, often second-guessing myself. The silence, combined with the emotional whiplash, left me stuck, feeling more isolated than ever. The start of his silent spells, as I recall, was tied to one of our most devastating breakups- a night that left me furious and heartbroken. I discovered that he had manipulated a woman into cosigning a car for him. At first, he tried to convince me it was purely a transactional arrangement, claiming he paid her for her signature. But the truth unraveled when I found out he was carrying on a full-blown relationship with her. The revelation didn't come gently- it slammed into me like the car he totaled the night before we were supposed to leave for a weekend trip. I remember the unease that woke me from my sleep, my eyes darting to the clock. The hours had slipped by, and he still hadn't shown up to my apartment. I tried calling his phone, each unanswered ring sending my heart into a tighter spiral of dread.

Finally, a text came, not his voice or his reassurance, just cold, dry instruction: "Cancel the hotel reservations. I have been in a wreck." No details, no explanation, just silence. Panic gripped me! My thoughts raced as I imagined the worst- was he hurt? Was he even alive? The hours that followed were a blur of frantic phone calls, enlisting friends and family to check hospitals, to scour for answers. My stomach was in knots, my pulse refusing to settle. The truth landed like a punch in the chest. He wasn't alone in the car. The other woman, the one he deceived into signing for the car, was with him. She was the one by his side, taking care of him while I was left in the dark.

When I finally reached him, trembling with a mix of relief and rage, he was indifferent, as though none of it mattered. His tone was flat, unbothered, and dismissive. He didn't try to understand why I was upset, as if this was normal behavior in his mind. The lack of remorse was chilling, and the emotional distance he maintained only deepened the wound. That night marked the beginning of a pattern. Silent spells that would punctuate our entire relationship, each one growing longer and more calculated. They carried with them a heavier weight of intimidation, laced with accusations and bursts of aggression, leaving me and my daughters walking on eggshells and questioning my sanity.

The Pity Play

A true master of manipulation, the narcissist knows when to turn the charm and intimidation to something more insidious: pity. This is the narcissist's secret weapon, the way they elicit sympathy from the protagonist. They will cast themselves as misunderstood and wounded.

The narcissist will give glimpses of supposed vulnerabilities, past trauma, or challenges they've had to "overcome." They may mention being betrayed by others, challenges that are never their fault, or struggles they only had to endure.

The pity play serves a dual purpose. First, it re-establishes control when the protagonist starts to pull away. Second, it is used to confuse the protagonist. They begin to feel guilty and empathetic, drawn by the desire to help or fix the narcissist. Pity-seeking ultimately is a power play to maintain their position and secure a fresh wave of emotional investment from those around them.

My protagonist wielded pity like a fine-tuned instrument, using it to play on my emotions and regain control. Looking back, it was his ultimate power play, a subtle but devastating weapon. In the beginning, he would recount the tragedies of his life with haunting detail, painting himself as the perpetual victim of others' cruelty. Most of his pain, he said, stemmed from his mother, whom he blamed for his failures and poor decisions. As he unraveled his story, his voice would carry a rehearsed cadence, a mix of anguish and bitterness that felt designed to draw sympathy.

His misfortunes became the justification for his bad decisions. Whenever he admitted to hurtful or questionable actions, he would pause, watching my face intently, his eyes scanning for judgment or approval. I didn't know it then, but these moments were tests. My responses were measured, empathetic, and nonjudgmental, serving as silent permission. Even when I disapproved, my lack of condemnation became implicit acceptance, a signal that I would endure his behavior without drawing hard boundaries. What I realize is that this was a way of vetting me, a way of gauging how far he could push and still keep me tethered.

After the initial breakup, I began to move forward with my life, determined to rebuild. I allowed him to visit our daughter, but I kept my distance emotionally. Yet when he discovered I was seeing someone new, the pity turned into an all-consuming strategy to reclaim what belonged to him. The calls and texts increased. He'd appear at my home unannounced, his face masked with sorrow, talking about how much he missed us and how he couldn't live without his family. His words are hollow, though; there was no genuine remorse, no acknowledgment of the pain he caused that led to our breakup.

Months later, when my apartment flooded and I needed temporary housing, he seized the opportunity. He offered us a place to stay with the pretense of generosity, promising it was only for stability until I found a new home. But it was only a calculated ploy to draw me back into his orbit. The arrangement was clear that we weren't back together, just coexisting temporarily. Yet, as the day approached for us to move out, his behavior was erratic. He manufactured an explosive argument about us leaving, accusing me of abandoning him again, twisting the narrative to cast himself as the victim.

Once we moved out, the messages started flooding in. Text after text, he'd send photos of himself with our daughter. Sending messages that read, *"Tell my daughter I love her, even if I'm not there with her."* Dripped with a mix of manipulation and guilt. His words were deliberate, designed to make me question whether I was breaking apart a family that could still be saved. Gifts arrived at my job:

flowers, poetry, and my favorite food, filled with empty promises and pleas for reconciliation. His outreach expanded beyond me. He went to those closest to me, enlisting them to plead his case, painting himself as the repentant man just wanting his family back.

I was caught in a web of his making; each thread spun with guilt, hope, and obligation. The pity he projected was suffocating, a constant reminder of the man he claimed to be versus the man I had come to know. The emotional toll was staggering. The waves of doubt, fleeting nostalgia, and sinking realization that this was not love but claims to ownership. Control disguised as desperation.

The Protagonist

A person in the Narcissist's orbit

"Charm is deceitful and beauty is passing, but a woman who fears the Lord, she shall be praised."

~ Proverbs 31:30 NKJV

Every play needs a protagonist, someone whose journey unfolds before the audience. The lamentable thing about it is that the protagonist in this play is not an actor willingly stepping into the spotlight, but someone inadvertently cast in the role. Drawn in by the Narcissist charm, and manipulation, the protagonist doesn't realize they are on stage until the story is well underway. By then, the lines are blurred, the exits are hidden, and the script seems to write itself. A script that traps them in cycles of hope, nostalgia, and guilt.

The curtain rises, and the Protagonist steps onto the stage and into a story already in motion. At first, they are swept up by grand gestures and promises that feel uniquely tailored. A dazzling adventure of shared dreams and partnership. Yet, behind the scenes, an intricate script unfolds, carefully orchestrated by the narcissist. Each moment is designed to bind the protagonist emotionally, fostering dependence on their approval and affection.

As the story progresses, the protagonist begins to feel the weight of their role. The initial glow of connection gives way to the harsh reality of the narcissist cycle of charm, devaluation, and silence. These patterns create an emotional muddle, leaving the protagonist disoriented and questioning their reality. Trapped in this orbit, they endure an unrelenting storm of highs and lows- moments of euphoric praise followed by cold detachment.

The toll is devastating, striking the protagonist in three pivotal aspects of their humanity. Emotional whiplash leaves the protagonists spinning, unsure of where they stand. Mental fog clouds their judgment, making it hard to discern the truth from manipulation. Lastly, isolation, carefully engineered by the narcissist, cuts the protagonist off from the outside world, leaving them vulnerable and alone.

Emotional Whiplash

The emotional whiplash inflicted by the narcissist is a deliberate tool of manipulation. With sudden and jarring shifts, they alternate between adoration and criticism, creating confusion and emotional instability. One moment, the protagonist is celebrated and cherished, and then the next, they are dismissed and punished. This calculated back-and-forth behavior is designed to erode self-confidence, instilling a sense of unworthiness that ties the Protagonist's value to the narcissist's ever-changing approval. The result is a relentless cycle that leaves the Protagonist questioning their reality and striving to regain fleeting moments of praise.

For me, this cycle found fertile ground in the aftermath of my second divorce, a period I now realize I did not properly grieve. A storm of emotions consumed me: sadness, anxiety, uncertainty, devastation, and frustration, all swirling beneath the surface while I outwardly tried to move on. Guilt and shame weighed heavily on me, as though the failure of the marriage was entirely mine to bear. But perhaps the most insidious part of my grief was the denial. I refused to acknowledge the depth of my pain, convincing myself that I could push past it, piece myself back together, and prove I was good.

Unbeknownst to me, these unresolved feelings left me vulnerable, searching for affirmation and connection. My heart was crying out for healing, but instead of seeking solace and guidance from God, I sought comfort through a person. When the narcissist entered my life, his attention and adoration felt like a lifeline. It was a way to fill the emptiness I was unwilling to confront. His charm distracted me from my brokenness, but it also tethered me to a cycle of manipulation that mirrored my inner turmoil.

By the time the jolts of his dismissive behavior began, I was already deeply entangled in the toxic dynamic. I found myself eager to please him and quick to shoulder the blame for his anger or withdrawal. Even when his toxic behavior caused the rift, I instinctively took responsibility, believing that if I worked harder, sacrificed more, or was simply "better," I could fix the fractures. My unresolved grief and lack of discernment left me chasing for his approval. Each attempt to regain his approval only tightened the chains of emotional dependence, pulling me further from the truth of who I was and from God, who longed to restore me.

Mental Fog

Over time, the protagonist begins to lose their sense of clarity. What once seemed obvious and straightforward now becomes shrouded in uncertainty. The narcissist's gaslighting tactics of denying events, twisting the truth, and outright blaming create doubt in the protagonist's perceptions of reality. The small whispers of doubt creep in and grow louder with each day. The once self-assured individual now questions their memories, instincts, and judgments. The narcissist distorts facts on the events that transpired. "That never happened," the narcissists insist, or "You're remembering it wrong," leaving the protagonist to wonder if their recollection is flawed. These moments of confusion, coupled with the narcissist's consistent dismissiveness, create a fog that clouds the protagonist's thoughts. They find themselves replaying conversations, seeking patterns, and trying to understand what went wrong, but the answers remain elusive.

The longer you remain in a relationship with the narcissists, the fog deepens. The protagonist becomes less confident in their ability to trust themselves. They second-guess their feelings, questioning whether their anger or hurt is justified or an overreaction. The internal struggle intensifies, as they try to reconcile with the person, they once were with the perplexed version of themselves they are becoming. The mental fog leaves the protagonist vulnerable, making it more difficult to escape the narcissist's grip.

The mental fog took me by surprise. I have always prided myself on my clarity of thought, my ability to see through deception, and my strong relationship with God, which I believed made me impervious to mental manipulation. But as the days went on, I found myself doubting my sanity. Small situations would arise, and he would always have an explanation for them. The first time I caught him, I found a woman's panties inside of his shorts while doing laundry. My stomach dropped as confusion and disbelief set in. I sent him a picture of what I found, and he responded with videos, claiming he attended a friend's party where there were strippers and insisted, he was unaware the panties were there. Every red flag in my mind was waving, but his explanation, paired with what felt like evidence, left me second-guessing myself. Maybe I was overreacting? I convinced myself to let it go, though a gnawing doubt lingered.

Another time, I discovered a provocative photo of him on his phone that he didn't share with me. When I asked him about the photo, he nonchalantly dismissed it, claiming that he was experimenting with something different but ultimately did like the result. Each incident chipped away at my confidence, making me question whether I was reading too much into things. The lies became more outrageous when I learned about his infidelity and the possibility of him fathering another child. He claimed that someone else pointed out the resemblance between him and the baby, presenting it to me not as a confession but as a casual question, leaving me bewildered and questioning the truth. Later in the relationship, there were moments when we made joint decisions, and he would later act as if those discussions had never happened or insist that he had the right to do whatever he wanted. I was losing my grip on reality, unsure if I could trust my judgment anymore.

I failed to set proper boundaries, allowing his manipulations to go unchecked. I ignored the red flags, convincing myself that I could handle it, that I could fix it somehow. I hid the truth from the people closest to me, not wanting them to see the chaos and confusion I was trapped in. I was embarrassed and ashamed, not wanting to admit that I was allowing myself to be manipulated. Each time I let it slide, I was silently complicit in my mental imprisonment.

Isolation

Isolation is a hallmark tactic of the narcissist, systematically executed to ensure their dominance over the protagonist. This process often begins subtly, with the narcissist planting seeds of doubt about the people in the protagonist's life. They create a sense of mistrust toward friends and family. Over time, these subtle remarks accumulate, leading the protagonist to question the intentions of their support network. As the relationship progresses, the isolation tactics become more explicit. The narcissist may actively discourage the protagonist from attending social events or speaking to loved ones. They may guilt trip the protagonist or create conflict, pitting the protagonist against friends and family. These actions ensure the protagonist becomes increasingly reliant on the narcissist for emotional support and validation, unaware of how their world is shrinking.

The stage is set for complete isolation when the protagonist finds themselves with no one to turn to. The narcissist has sabotaged key relationships, by sowing discord or by monopolizing the protagonist's time and energy. Isolation serves two purposes for the narcissist: it removes external perspectives that could challenge the narcissist's control and fosters a dependence where the protagonist feels trapped in the relationship.

My experience with isolation began subtly and took hold later in the relationship, though the groundwork was much earlier. At the start of our relationship, the world was already in a state of isolation, which created an unusual dynamic. My relationships with my immediate family were strained, and sharing my struggles with them didn't feel like an option. The tension in my family relationships had been a common issue that my narcissist and I shared. Similarly, past experiences with romantic relationships made me hesitant to share details with friends, fearing they might form negative opinions of him if we stayed together.

In the beginning, he embraced my friends and church community, even creating separate relationships with them that seemed genuine at the time. He was invited to birthday parties, and private celebrations, attended church regularly with me, and would often cook for my friends, seemingly supportive of connections with others. I had no idea that, later, he would attempt to use these same connections to manipulate and gain access to me again. The shift toward isolation became apparent after we were engaged and moved in together. If I planned to go out while he stayed home, he would make me feel guilty, as though leaving the house was an act of neglect toward him. Ironically, he was rarely home, coming and going as he pleased without explanation or accountability.

The control extended to my friendships. He questioned my close bond with my best friend, a male he had seen me spend time with frequently. He claimed he was no longer comfortable with us hanging out, suggesting my friend had ulterior motives and wanted to be more than friends. He also became critical of another male friend, a trusted confidant who, along with his wife, we had chosen as godparents for our child. He insisted I stop confiding in him about my struggles, particularly anything related to him or our relationship. As if that wasn't enough, he went further, trying to make me question the loyalty of my close-knit friend circle. He seemed to know specific details about private conversations we'd had, claiming that my friends were sharing these discussions with him and accusing them of betraying my trust. He planted seeds of doubt, attempting to convince me that I couldn't rely on my friends and that their allegiance was questionable. This tactic might have worked if I hadn't discovered that he cloned my phone and was reading the messages exchanged in our group text.

Even my children became a source of tension. He grew jealous when I spent time with them or focused on their activities instead of prioritizing him. The guilt and explicit accusations left me feeling torn, as though nurturing my existing relationships and being present for my children was somehow a betrayal of him.

Due to my lack of confidence and brokenness, I feared being alone, which made me feel obligated to prioritize him above all else. When I wasn't putting him first, I felt inadequate as his partner. I found myself constantly readjusting plans and bending to his guilt trips, unsure of how to assert my own needs. The turning point for me, the moment I call my "awakening," came during a trip to visit friends who lived in another state. As the weekend went on, I began to feel safe enough to open up about everything I was experiencing. Not only did they listen without judgment, but they also held me accountable, offering some hard truths about the damage I was doing to myself by staying in that relationship. It was during this time that I realized this trip wasn't just a coincidence. It was God's way of getting my attention, giving me the space and clarity I needed to see the truth. That trip marked the beginning of my realization that I deserved more than the isolation and manipulation I had been living with.

Reflective Intermission

Taking Inventory

Emotional:

1. Reflect on any past experiences where you felt emotionally caught in cycles of praise and criticism. How did those shifts affect your sense of worth and emotional stability?
2. Think about whether you have avoided processing past emotional hurt. How has this affected your ability to form healthy connections in your life?
3. Reflect on a time when you felt emotionally uncertain or questioned your instincts. How did it affect your emotional state and decision-making?

Mental:

4. Think of a time when you struggled with mental fog in relationships. How do you deal with situations that make you second-guess yourself?

5. Reflect on times when you ignored red flags or excused behaviors that didn't feel right. What led you to rationalize or overlook these behaviors?
6. Consider times when you questioned whether your feelings or reactions were "too much" or overblown. How do you navigate the mental disarray caused by doubt?

Spiritual:

7. Reflect on whether you have felt compelled to stay in a relationship or sacrifice your needs for the sake of the relationship. How did God's presence (or absence) shape your sense of worth and validation during that time?
8. Reflect on how refusing to acknowledge your pain and brokenness may have kept you from seeking God's healing. How did this denial contribute to your emotional and spiritual vulnerability?
9. Reflect on whether you have ever bypassed spiritual insight when faced with warning signs of toxicity. What

prevented you from addressing those feelings sooner?

The Supporting Cast

The "Flying Monkeys"

"Do not incline my heart to (consent to or tolerate) any evil thing, or to practice deeds of wickedness with men who plan and do evil; let me not eat of their delicacies (be tempted by their gain)."

~ Psalm 141:4

In the play of narcissist manipulation, the narcissist doesn't work alone. They rely on a supporting cast of enablers and "flying monkeys" - people who, whether knowingly or unknowingly, help to further the narcissist agenda. These individuals can be friends, family, or even strangers, but all share one thing in common: they fall under the narcissist's spell. Some are manipulated through charm, drawn in by the narcissist's ability to appear charismatic and charming, while others are coerced by fear, guilt, or a sense of obligation.

Enablers, either consciously or unconsciously, support narcissist behavior, creating an environment where manipulation, deceit, and control can thrive. They may ignore or rationalize harmful behavior, excusing the narcissist's actions and reinforcing the status quo. Narcissists will use charm and flattery, making enablers feel important and needed, bolstering loyalty. They'll play the victim, painting themselves as misunderstood or mistreated, to win sympathy and support. Guilt and fear are also used as tools. The narcissist will make the enablers feel responsible for their well-being or suggest that something terrible will happen if they don't comply.

Flying monkeys, on the other hand, are actively recruited to do the narcissist bidding. They act as messengers, spies, or even attackers, used strategically to undermine the protagonist, and isolate them from their support network, or spread false narratives that maintain the narcissist power.

Additionally, the narcissist creates a divide between people, encouraging enablers and "flying monkeys" to take sides or act as intermediaries, further isolating the protagonist from their support system. They will manipulate information, sharing distorted versions of events that serve their narrative while making others lie about the truth. The narcissist may also promise rewards, like affection or recognition, to those who align with them, while punishing those who don't.

What makes the role of the enabler and flying monkey particularly dangerous is the emotional hold the narcissist has over them. Whether through charm or fear, these individuals are often unaware that they are playing a part in the narcissist toxic drama, and their actions, no matter how small, serve to fuel the emotional whiplash, mental fog, and isolation, the disempowerment of the protagonist.

The roles played in my story were so convoluted that I couldn't fully unravel them until I had broken free from the Narcissist grip. Even now, I can't definitively account for everyone in cahoots with him. I may never uncover the full network of enablers and flying monkeys. But one thing I do know: the community I once called family, the one I introduced him to, was completely shattered—people who had once stood by me, walking with me through some of the hardest seasons of my life, dismissed my cries for help. Their responses stung in ways I wasn't prepared for.

Time and time again, I was told, “He would never hurt you,” or “He’s not that crazy; he knows we know him.” The pain of the words lingered, not just because they invalidated my reality, but because they came from people I trusted with my heart.

Then, some chose to remain neutral, as if neutrality in the face of danger was an option. Their indifference, though likely meant to avoid conflict, placed me and my daughter in harm’s way. The heartbreak of cutting ties with people I loved and believed loved me in return was almost unbearable, but it was necessary for our safety.

And then there were the flying monkeys. These individuals, under his sway, operated in a haze of charm and fear. He kept them close enough to manipulate, yet distant enough to avoid their scrutiny. Even his family members, those who knew of his manipulative tendencies and violent history, stayed silent. They normalized his behavior, brushing off his actions as if they were part of everyday life.

Looking back, the betrayal from all sides felt like a series of sharp cuts, each one deepening the wound. But through the pain, I’ve learned to listen to the voice of God that is my true north. I've learned that my safety and the safety of my children are worth more than maintaining appearances or connections. And while the scars of those relationships remain, they now serve as a reminder of the strength it took to walk away and the boundaries I've built to protect my peace.

This chapter is not intended to ridicule or blame, but rather to serve as a cautionary measure to raise awareness and shed light on the fact that enablers or "flying monkeys" are being used and manipulated just as much as the protagonist. Too often, toxic behavior is overlooked, dismissed as a personality trait, or the seriousness of the situation is minimized. My prayer is that the knowledge shared in this chapter helps you recognize if you have fallen into one of these roles, encouraging you to reflect and choose not to participate in the narcissist's schemes. In doing so, the destructive plans of the enemy can be thwarted before causing irreparable harm.

The Climax

Breaking Free and Claiming the Stage

"He gives power to the weak, and to those who have no might, He increases strength. Even the youths shall faint and be weary, and the young men shall utterly fall, but those that wait on the Lord shall renew their strength; They shall mount up on wings like eagles, they shall run and not be weary, they shall run and not faint."

~ Isaiah 40:29-31

The protagonist had been cast in a role, not of their choosing. A role carefully designed to diminish their voice and identity. The protagonist was the compliant partner, the quiet peacekeeper, the one who absorbed the tension to maintain the illusion of harmony. While the narcissist commanded the spotlight, the protagonist was relegated to the shadows, their lines dictated by a script they never agreed to.

Each act of the performance chipped away at their spirit. The script demanded silence, sacrifice, and unquestioning loyalty, while the narcissist kept the stage under tight control. The supporting cast- enablers, and the "flying monkeys" reinforced the narrative, their actions blurring the lines between loyalty and complicity. To the protagonist, it felt as though the world was conspiring to keep them in their assigned role, a role that grew heavier with every passing scene.

The cracks in the production began to show as the protagonist's awareness grew. They started to see the stage for what it truly was: a carefully constructed illusion meant to maintain the narcissist power. The protagonist recognizes the tools of manipulation- guilt, gaslighting, love bombing, fear- woven into the script to keep them in place. This recognition was the first spark of rebellion, a quiet yet profound realization that the role that they had been playing was not their true self.

The climax came like the turning of a page. In a moment of defiance, the protagonist stepped out of the shadows and into the center of the stage. They no longer followed the script that kept them bound. This act was not a loud or chaotic scene but one of deliberate strength and clarity.

The protagonist spoke truths that had been long buried, cutting through the web of lies spun by the narcissist. The flying monkeys and enablers, so accustomed to the protagonist's compliance, faltered. The power dynamics shifted as the protagonist refused to play their part any longer.

The stage, once a place of confinement, now stood as a platform for transformation. Where shadows once loomed, light began to break through, illuminating the path to freedom. The protagonist no longer stumbled through a script written by someone else. Instead, they began to rewrite their lines- bold, unapologetic, and true. The scars they carried were no longer marks of defeat but emblems of resilience, each one a testament to battles fought and survived, a reminder of their strength to endure and rise.

For me, my climax mirrored the protagonist. My turning point came on May 17, 2023, during my quiet, sacred time with God. In the stillness of the morning, pen to journal, He guided my pen to draw a line. A seemingly simple act but one that would redefine everything. Above the line was a dot representing myself, and the word *Me* representing Christ. Below the line, we have one word: "him," which stands for the narcissist.

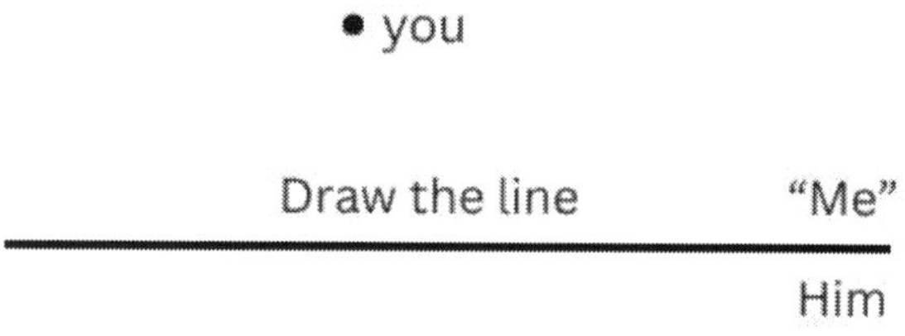

• you

Draw the line "Me"

Him

Then God spoke words to me that pierced through the hard places of my heart. "This is a line of demarcation. You are separate, not equal. You have been walking through this life together but on different sides of the line. Above the line is one of availability. Here, you are more than a conqueror with unlimited resources. The yoke is easy, and the burden is light. Few walk above the line because many are unaware of the abundance and access, they have with Me. Below the line is survival- a place of scarcity, with limited resources and no access to Me. Below, they are weighed down by the yoke of bondage."

His words were both a rebuke and an invitation. I realized that I had been tethered to a life of scarcity, where my worth was dictated by someone who thrived on my brokenness.

But now God was showing me that I could step back. I didn't have to play this role anymore. The curtain could fall on this chapter, and I could allow Him to rewrite my story, not as a victim trapped in someone else's tragedy, but as a warrior rising in truth and grace.

Slowly, I began to reclaim my life. It wasn't an instant transformation but a series of deliberate, painful, and holy choices. God gave me specific instructions for freedom, each one a step closer to breaking the chains that held me. I set boundaries where there had been none. I spoke truths that had long been silenced. I started prioritizing my needs, not as acts of selfishness, but as declarations of worth.

When I started to rise, he fought back hard. At first, he tried to charm me, but when that didn't work, he turned cold—silent and disrespectful. He accused me of things I never did, questioning my loyalty every time I went out alone. It felt like he was trying to strip away my dignity, speaking to me like a child, attacking my character. He even demanded everything he'd ever given me back, telling me I was nothing without him. The more I stepped into my freedom, the more his façade crumbled. Truths that had been hidden in the dark began to surface, each revelation a nail in the coffin of our toxic dynamic. Exiting the relationship was not the dramatic, triumphant moment I had once imagined. It was a series of quiet rebellions, several small acts of courage, and obedience to God's voice. With every step, I peeled back layers of control he had wrapped around me. I rediscovered the person I had been all along- the one that was forgotten in the chaos. I am strong in Christ. I am an overcomer! I am bold and courageous. I am worthy of love and respect. The stage is now mine, no longer a place of confinement but a sanctuary of truth and redemption.

Inside-Out Acting

The spirits behind narcissism

"Put on the whole armor of God, that you may be able to stand against the wiles of the devil. For we do not wrestle against flesh and blood, but against principalities, against powers, against rulers of the darkness of this age, against spiritual hosts of wickedness in the heavenly places."

~ Ephesians 6:11-12 NKJV

We have come to the heart of why this book must be written. As I walk with Christ, I've come to understand that the battles we face are not simply physical or interpersonal but deeply spiritual. We are called to remain vigilant, not just for our own sake, but to recognize the enemy's schemes in the world around us.

Peter, an apostle of Christ, reminds us of this urgency:

"Be sober [well balanced and self-disciplined], be alert and cautious at all times. That enemy of yours, the devil, prowls around like a roaring lion [fiercely hungry],

seeking someone to devour. But resist him, be firm in your faith [attack his attack-rooted established, immovable], knowing that the same experience by your brothers and sisters throughout the world. [You do not suffer alone.]" (1 Peter 5:8-9, AMP)

Through my journey, I've gained a deeper revelation of what it truly means to keep the commandments of God. They are not simply rules to follow; they are safeguards, divine principles meant to protect us from the snares and traps laid by the enemy. This is how we resist him with obedience and intentionality.

Narcissistic behavior is one such snare, often appearing as a battle in the physical realm but originating from a spiritual and psycho-emotional condition. It's far greater and more insidious than it seems on the surface. To understand it fully, we must look deeper, beyond the external actions, and explore the inner world that motivates these behaviors.

This is where the concept of "Inside-out acting" becomes crucial. In theater, this technique focuses on understanding a character's internal psycho-emotional condition and their motives, which then drive their outward behaviors. Similarly, in understanding narcissistic behavior, we must dig deeper into the inner turmoil, wounds, insecurities, and self-distorted perceptions that fuel their outward manipulation, control, charm, and the forces behind it.

To fully comprehend the spiritual implications of narcissistic behavior, it's important to explore a few foundational terms: legal rights, strongman, and strongholds. These terms not only help us recognize how demonic influences gain access but also shed light on the spiritual warfare at play.

A **legal right** refers to the spiritual "rules" or principles that govern the spirit realm. When we violate these principles through sin, unforgiveness, or other actions, it grants demonic spirits the authority to harass, oppress, or remain in us.

A **strongman** is a ruling spirit, a demonic entity that holds authority over a specific area of bondage (stronghold). This is referenced in Psalm 91:5-6, where the terrors of the night and arrows by day hint at these ruling forces.

A **stronghold** is a fortified place in a person's mind or soul where Satan exalts himself against the knowledge of God. Scripture speaks of this in 2 Corinthians 10:4-

5: *"For the weapons are not carnal but mighty in God for pulling down strongholds, casting down arguments and every high thing that exalts itself against the knowledge of God."*

Now, let's look at how these concepts apply to narcissistic behavior. Narcissism often involves spiritual strongholds deeply rooted in pride, manipulation, and control, traits that mirror the influence of ruling spirits. Demonic spirits gain access through various "open doors." Here are just a few ways the doors can be opened:

Sin- both personal and ancestral (generational)

Soul ties- unhealthy emotional and physical connections (fornication, adultery, sexual impurity)

Demonic vows- agreements made consciously or unconsciously (occult or cults)

Unforgiveness- that festers and gives way to bitterness

Childhood rejection- where wounds from neglect, abandonment, or lack of affirmation create fertile ground for insecurity and spiritual oppression

Points of weakness- moments of despair or trauma

Spoken self (word) curses or destructive inner vows.

Cursed Objects bring spiritual oppression to one's life.

This list isn't exhaustive, but it highlights how demonic spirits gain access to influence a person's life. When it comes to narcissistic behavior, there are 8 dominant spirits often at work, each contributing to the emotional, mental, and spiritual turmoil characteristic of narcissism. Below, we'll explore these spirits in detail and how they manifest. Please note, they are listed in no particular order.

1. **Spirit of Witchcraft**

   Often associated with the occult, witches, warlocks, black magic, white magic, charms, psychics, and horoscopes, this spirit manifests manipulation and rebellion. Sometimes called the "Delilah Spirit," the master manipulator seeks to control others through deceit. *(1 Samuel 15:23)*

2. **Spirit of Envy**

Characterized by resentful dissatisfaction over what another person has, this spirit fosters feelings of entitlement and jealousy. Attached to it are spirits of covetousness, hatred, and rage. It manifests as spite, revenge, cruelty, murder, kleptomania (theft), material lust, greed, discontentment, suspicion, distrust, and selfishness. *(Proverbs 14:30)*

3. **Spirit of Confusion**

This spirit creates mental and emotional distraction and disorientation, paralyzing and overwhelming its victims to the point of questioning God and their sanity. It often shows up as blame shifting, love bombing, avoidance and praise, and refusal to accept accountability. *(1 Corinthians 14:33)*

4. **Spirit of Condemnation**

This spirit is all about making people feel hopeless. It works through accusations that are meant to tear others down, always finding something wrong with them. You'll notice it showing up as deflection, criticism, and shifting the blame onto someone else. (*Romans 8:1-4)*

5. **Spirit of Control (Jezebel Spirit)**

Known for controlling the narrative by any means necessary, this spirit employs mental and emotional tricks to dominate. It manifests through sarcasm, put-downs, and tactics designed to make others feel unworthy or inadequate. *(1 Kings 16-2 Kings 9)*

6. **Spirit of Deception (Lying Spirit)**

This spirit thrives in falsehoods, exaggerating its own qualities while diminishing others. It often brings religious bondage, superstitions, false prophecies, accusations, gossip, slander, and false teaching. *(Proverbs 12:22, 2 Corinthians 10:12)*

7. **Spirit of Pride**

This narcissistic trait, also known as the Leviathan spirit, is built on arrogance and self-importance. It shows up in behaviors like boastfulness, impatience, stubbornness, self-righteousness, entitlement (including a victim mentality), and an inflated sense of superiority. *(Job 41, Luke 14:11)*

8. **Spirit of Fear**

Beneath the narcissist's false persona lies an underpinning of overwhelming anxiety and worry born from a lack of faith and trust in God. While they appear confident, charismatic, and charming, this disguise often masks an insecure and immature inner self. *(Joshua 1:9, 1 John 4:18, 2 Timothy 1:7, Job 3:25-26)*

The purpose of exposing these spirits is not for you to attempt to deliver individuals yourself, as deliverance is a voluntary action and a personal commitment to God. Rather, it is to shed light on the enemy's schemes and to bring awareness to potential "open doors" that may exist in your own life.

This knowledge serves as a call to repentance and rededication, or for those who have yet to take this step, to accept God as your Lord and Savior where true safety and freedom are found.

To anyone who finds themselves in this type of relationship, or if you see these behaviors manifesting around you, ask God for a way of escape. And if you realize that you are the one exhibiting these behaviors, know this: it is not too late for you. If you've found this book, take it as a divine opportunity. Run to God, surrender your life to Him, and allow Him to transform you from the inside out!

For my fellow intercessors and watchmen on the wall, let these truths guide your prayers and intercessions. For the entire community of believers, let this knowledge sober your mind, awaken your spirit, and keep you vigilant in the face of spiritual warfare.

Curtain Speech

The Conclusion

"Do not fear (anything), for I am with you; Do not be afraid, for I am your God. I will strengthen you, be assured I will help you; I will certainly take hold of you with My righteous right hand (a hand of justice, of power, of victory, of salvation)"

~ Isaiah 41:10

The journey hasn't been easy; it's been filled with tears, heartache, and moments when I didn't think I'd make it. But every step has been both necessary and worth it. When I was in that relationship, I felt trapped in a darkness so thick that I couldn't see a way out. It wasn't until I surrendered everything to God—my fears, my brokenness, my hope for freedom—that I began to see His light breaking through.

Since that season, I've encountered countless others who have endured similar pain. Some have found their way to healing, while others' stories remind us of the weight of staying silent and unseen.

As you turn these pages, I pray that my testimony speaks to the deepest parts of your heart. May it remind you that no matter how heavy the burden is, you are never too far from God's reach. I hope that you allow Him to step into your story, to guide you toward freedom, healing, and the fullness of life He has planned for you. This book contains just a glimpse of my journey, but everything I am and everything I do now belongs to Him. His plans for me and you are perfect, even when the road feels impossible.

As you turn to the final page, I invite you to take a step of faith—a call to salvation or rededication. Whether you are clinging to hope by a thread or standing on the edge of renewal, know this: God's love is relentless, His grace is sufficient, and His arms are wide open, ready to welcome you home.

A Call to Salvation or Rededication

God is calling you into a personal relationship with Him or renew the one you may have drifted away from. This is a moment to embrace His love, grace, and forgiveness.

Here are key truths to guide you:

Acknowledgment of God's Love and Grace

God loves you unconditionally. His grace is a gift freely given to all who believe.

"For God so [greatly] loved and dearly prized the world, that He [even] gave His [One and] only begotten Son, that whoever believes and trusts in Him [as Savior] shall not perish but have eternal life." **(John 3:16 AMP)**

"But God clearly shows and proves His love for us, by the fact that while we were yet sinners, Christ died for us." **(Romans 5:8 AMP)**

Recognition of sin and the need for repentance

Every person has fallen short of God's standard

"Since all have sinned and continually fall short of the glory of God." **(Romans 3:23 AMP)**

Turning to God requires repentance, which means changing your mind and direction, leaving behind sinful ways. *"So repent [change your inner self, your old way of thinking, regret past sins] and return [to God -seek His purpose for your life], so that your sins may be wiped away [blotted out, completely erased,] so that times of refreshing may come from the presence of the Lord [restoring you like a cool wind on a hot day]"* **(Acts 3:19)**

Faith and Confession

Salvation comes through faith in Jesus Christ.

"If you acknowledge and confess with your mouth that Jesus is Lord [recognizing His power, authority, and majesty as God] and believe in your heart that God raised Him from the dead, you will be saved." **(Romans 10:9 AMP)**

The Power of Forgiveness and New Life

God forgives all sins and offers a fresh start:

"If we [freely] admit that we have sinned and confess our sins, He is faithful and just [true to His own nature and promises] and will forgive our sins and cleanse us continually from all unrighteousness [our wrongdoing, everything not in conformity with His will and purpose]" **(1 John 1:9 AMP)**

Therefore, if anyone is in Christ [that is grafted in, joined to Him by faith in Him as Savior], he is a new creature [reborn, renewed by the Holy Spirit]; old things [the previous moral and spiritual condition] have passed away. Behold, new things have come [because spiritual awakening brings a new life]. (2 Corinthians 5:17 AMP)

Encouragement to Rededicate

If you have drifted away, God is ready to welcome you back: Pray this prayer from Psalm 51 to rededicate to God.

"Create in me a clean heart, O God, and renew a right and steadfast spirit within me. Do not cast me away from Your presence and do not take Your Holy Spirit from me. Restore to me the joy of Your salvation and sustain me with a willing spirit." (Psalm 51:10-12 AMP)

Thank you for your loving kindness towards me. In Jesus name, Amen.

Call to Salvation

Take a moment to say this prayer of salvation:

> *"God, I come to You recognizing my need for Your love and forgiveness. I confess that I have sinned, and I turn away from my old ways. I believe that Jesus died for my sins and rose again so that I may have eternal life. Today, I surrender my life to You. I ask You to come into my heart, guide me, and make me new. Thank*

you for Your mercy and grace. In Jesus name, Amen."

If you said either of those prayers, I'm so excited for you! The angels in heaven are celebrating your decision right now. (Luke 15:10)

Next Steps

Take time to pray, read and study the Bible, and connect with others who share your faith. Whether it's through a church or a small group, finding fellowship will help you grow. As you embrace your journey with God, trust in His promises and guidance every step of the way.

Made in the USA
Columbia, SC
28 April 2025

57167771R00041